# 7 Steps to a Life of Serendipity

*Serendipity*

Edited by:
Alisha Squip
Deanna L. Matheuszik

Book Formatting: Write on Promotions

Cover by: Photograph by:
Write on Promotions
Printed and manufactured in the United States of America.
ISBN: 9798866071586
Registered with the Library of Congress.

Most discoveries, even today, are a combination of Serendipity and of Searching.

~Siddhartha Mukherjee

This book is dedicated to all the beautiful people who fight inner shadows and seek peace, happiness, and Serendipity.

Thank you to Irene, Freddie, Lori, Eightball, Jani, Carlos Woods, Illdiko Basa, Nicola Mitchell, Jackie Garcia, and to all my precious Serendips

Alisha Squip - Editor
Deanna L. Matheuszik, Ph.D. -Editor

.

# Table of Contents

# Step 1:
# Understanding a
# Life of Serendipity

# Understanding a Life of Serendipity

We live life between two poles: positivity and negativity. Most of our physical experiences are a roller-coaster of mixed emotions and feelings, while we genuinely strive to reach a bright and cheerful perspective so we can have a contented life.

All of us encounter serendipitous moments in life. Still, only a few can transform such energy encounters into lighthouses to guide us and show us our next steps. Only a few understand the secret of living a life of Serendipity—this 7-week shadow work transformation journal walks you through the process, Step by Step. Let's get started.

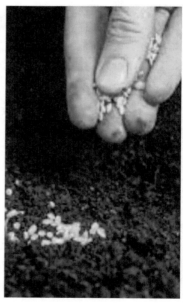

I am excited to outline how I recognize this form of energy and have made it an integral part of my life. See, Serendipity brings serenity into your life, enabling you to appreciate the miracle of your existence, understand your Starseed, and create a balance between negative and positive. Once you know a Life of Serendipity, you will unexpectedly receive the secret that opens up the treasure of spiritual, emotional, physical, and material contentment. The only thing needed to attain Serendipity is an attitude of gratefulness and willingness to trust the process outlined step by step in this course.

Although Serendipity has been in our lives since the beginning of time, the word itself entered our dictionary in the eighteenth century. Before the term got its meaning, serendipitous events were passed as events that happen purely by chance. Serendipity was never considered a stand-alone divine energy life force. Serendipity is like a turbo boost or a charging chariot. Serendipity comprises the elements of visions, signs, symbols, chance, luck, peace, destiny, blessings, and miracles. This surge of energy is always in motion gushing around, waiting to settle, nest, and expand. So, how can you harness a turbo boost?

A British historian, Horace Walpole, delved into the concept of Serendipity and how it affects our lives. He found inspiration in "The Travels and Adventures of Three Princes of Serendip," a Persian fable that recounts the exploits of three princes on the island of Serendip, now known as Sri Lanka.

These princes embarked on a journey to expand their knowledge beyond the conventional academic learning and narrow-minded views of the royal court, per their father, King Jafar's orders. With their sharp observational skills and adventurous spirit, they stumbled upon Serendipity.

Walpole described this unique form of learning: "The princes were always making discoveries by chance and using their wisdom to understand things that they weren't even searching for." He defined Serendipity as the life-altering intersection between a purposeful journey, a desire for profound knowledge, and a universal alignment.

(Horace Walpole to Sir Horace Mann, 28 January 1754 in The Yale Edition of Horace Walpole's Correspondence, ed. W. S. Weis (Yale University Press, 1937 1983), vol. 20, pp 407 11).

Encountering someone who brings out the best in you and fills you with positive emotions is an example of serendipity. Although these moments are common in life, we often fail to recognize their true value and dismiss them as something unusual, irrational, or too good to be true. We have a tendency to overlook these magical moments due to our narrow-mindedness. We are yet to discover the potential of utilizing these moments to improve our lives. This study guide aims to change that. It will teach you how to experience the wonderful blessings of Serendipity on a deeper level and use them to your advantage.

The key to experiencing Serendipity is to connect with your heart space or heart chakra. It is imperative to live a serendipitous lifestyle. If you are going through emotional turmoil such as heartbreak, grief, low self-esteem, or lack of self-love, this course will help you achieve emotional "heart" health and wholeness. Remember, our heart plays a significant role in experiencing serendipitous moments.

A life full of Serendipity improves the present by adding gratification and happiness in shaping your future.

Most people who purchase or receive this study guide are at the crossroads of their lives and possibly feeling stuck. Do you feel like you are in a rut or want to run away from yourself or your current situation? Well, this is where your "shadow work" begins.

Shadow work is a self-proclamation that might go something like this: "All the things I thought I knew about myself are not making sense anymore, and I need to change how I think and how I lead my life; but how do I start? I realize it's up to me, and I am ready to change. I need help!"

Shadow work is working on the unpleasant parts of your personality and behavior, holding you from reaching your full potential. The first self-examination or self-assessment is never easy, But if you 1. trust the process, 2. understand the concept, and 3. do the work, you will enjoy a new perspective and live a bright, more cheerful, and content life.

Only when you welcome change, big or small, can you understand the concept of Serendipity.

Life is a journey, not a moment. Traveling on life's windy roads with a dark and negative mindset eventually leads to nothingness, numbness, and loneliness. But suppose you can learn to purify your vision and look at the unique ways life transforms serendipitous events into a positive, growth-oriented outlook. In that case, it will make your life excellent and adventurous.

To live a Life of Serendipity, all you need to do is recognize and cherish Serendipity the moment it happens. Serendipity is beneficial when you see/recognize it and use it within the context in which it occurs. This application of Serendipity is vital as it can lead to the breakthrough you seek in your personal life.

Serendipity is already in your life; that's the great part! But she only appears once you live a purpose-driven life. Understanding Serendipity gives you an advantage in your own composition of your life. That's why the unique things around you are all happening for you to achieve your goals, so hang on for the ride.

It takes a clear personal self-evaluation to discover the treasures hidden deep within your existence.

You will feel like a detective looking for clues. Suddenly, you acknowledge that all coincidences are a series of divine occurrences working together for your higher good.

Once your vision is on the lookout for unique occurrences, you will see symbols, signals, and signs of Serendipity in your life. Realizing them takes a crystal clear outlook through focus and discipline. As you see, Serendipity is a mindset, a perspective, and an open heart aware of every nuance of your existence.

Once you see the simple blessings in the air you breathe or show your gratefulness for a tiny bee pollinating a daisy, you have set the wheels of fortune churning, and Serendipity will begin to shower you with unforeseen gifts.

All you need is to take a leap of faith and follow the path of your dreams. Your life journey will be full of twists and turns, ups and downs, but your goals, once defined, will be more significant than all your fears.

It may require courage and a motivational push, but the universe sends symbols, signals, and signs. These symbols, signals, and signs enter your life as a surprise, sometimes in the darkest hours and sometimes in the brightest times. The art of recognizing and embracing them leads to a life of utmost Serendipity. A serendipitous moment attracts a turbo boost of multiple moments that enormously impact your life. The way forward might not be comprehensible at first, but the fortune brought by Serendipity will become evident in time. All you need is to be daring enough to acknowledge the significance of Serendipity and shake hands with what the future will bring!

With practice, understanding the signs of Serendipity becomes much more accessible. The positive vibes emanating from Serendipity will help clear your cluttered mind. People you meet by chance will spark an energy you have long sought to find. This is how you bring fortune into your life, from places you least expect or didn't expect at all!

# 7 Day Meditation
## EXERCISE

Our lives can become excessively hectic, causing us to neglect *being*. We should learn to resist social media, work, and family pressures and expectations and make time each day to allow our bodies and minds to relax. Failing to do so can cause us to overlook moments of Serendipity.

Slowing down and unwinding to benefit your mental and physical well-being is crucial. These relaxing activities are helpful. Whether reading a few pages of a new book, taking a warm bath, or watching your favorite TV show. However, it's important to regularly incorporate deep relaxation into your routine for genuine bodily, psychological, and spiritual rejuvenation.

Meditation is a great way to achieve deep relaxation and has several physiological benefits. It can lower your heart rate, blood pressure, and muscle tension. It also helps reduce anxiety, improve concentration and memory, and boost self-confidence.

To start this meditation practice, please read the following three paragraphs slowly. While doing so, try to visualize yourself exercising in your mind.

# 7 Day Meditation
## EXERCISE

Take a moment to relax and clear your mind of any worries or troubles. Think back to a joyful memory, such as a cherished moment with a loved one or a special event that brought you happiness. Focus on this memory and allow it to make you smile. Hold onto this feeling and allow it to fill you with joy and happiness. Focus on that memory over and over till you do not need the memory to experience the feeling.

Now, you can flip this feeling from the past memory and shift/attach it to a vision you have for yourself in the future; next, bring that future vision of yourself with the feeling of the past memory into your present meditation. This exercise is like brain pushups, and it may be challenging at first, but it's how you change your mindset. Embrace the discomfort within the practice as you try and try again and use it to propel yourself toward the future you desire.

To access your guided meditation, scan the provided QR code.

# Shadow Work Subsciption

Purchase a 7-day pink candle to promote harmony and joy while dissipating negativity in your living space.

Try a Dream Satchel with a Rose Quartz Crystal, Rose Petals, Lavender, and Jasmine.

To further enhance your well-being, consider taking Nature's Sunshine "Open Heart."
Flower Essence drops.

Scan the QR code
for more information.

Lastly, a sage smudge sticks to purify yourself and your living space. This is important as you will expel spiritual, emotional, and physical energy. Make sure to smudge with closed doors and windows, walk clockwise in your space, then open all windows and doors and let the smoke be sucked out into the outdoors. Also, begin to smudge visitors when they come into your closed space.

# Before you
## begin your Gratitude Journal

Start your day by doing this simple stretching and focusing exercise daily before beginning your daily tasks. It's a minor exercise that helps ground you and clear your mind. Sit straight in your chair with your feet flat on the floor and close your eyes. Slowly take five deep breaths to ease any tension.

Next, while breathing, rotate your shoulder blades upward and backward in a rhythm, counting up to ten slowly and gently. This exercise will help you release any negative thoughts.

Finally, reverse the rotation, starting with your shoulders up and moving forward until you reach the number ten again. As you feel your muscles and energy relax, your mind will clear, allowing you to focus on your day's tasks.

_____

# Gratitude Journal

s    m    t    w    t    f    s

Date :

My Cards for the day                  Today I'm grateful for

Schedule                              Hope

☐ _____        ☐ _____

☐ _____        ☐ _____

☐ _____        ☐ _____

☐ _____        ☐ _____

Notes

# Gratitude Journal

s  m  t  w  t  f  s

Date :

### My Cards for the day

### Today I'm grateful for

### Schedule

☐ _____
☐ _____
☐ _____
☐ _____

### Hope

☐ _____
☐ _____
☐ _____
☐ _____

### Notes

# Gratitude Journal

s    m    t    w    t    f    s

Date :

My Cards for the day

Today I'm grateful for

Schedule

☐ _____
☐ _____
☐ _____
☐ _____

Hope

☐ _____
☐ _____
☐ _____
☐ _____

Notes

# Gratitude Journal

s     m     t     w     t     f     s

Date :

### My Cards for the day

### Today I'm grateful for

### Schedule

☐ _____
☐ _____
☐ _____
☐ _____

### Hope

☐ _____
☐ _____
☐ _____
☐ _____

### Notes

# Gratitude Journal

s   m   t   w   t   f   s

Date :

My Cards for the day

Today I'm grateful for

Schedule

☐ _____
☐ _____
☐ _____
☐ _____

Hope

☐ _____
☐ _____
☐ _____
☐ _____

Notes

# Gratitude Journal

s    m    t    w    t    f    s

Date :

### My Cards for the day

### Today I'm grateful for

### Schedule

- [ ] _____
- [ ] _____
- [ ] _____
- [ ] _____

### Hope

- [ ] _____
- [ ] _____
- [ ] _____
- [ ] _____

### Notes

# Step 2: Serendipity in Relation with Self

## Serendipity in Relationship with Self

The self, or your ego, is the essence of your whole existence, and it is shaped by what you experience—the triumphs you achieve and the struggles you endure. Your demeanor, perspective, attitude towards life, and everything that happens to you and around you determine whether you have a healthy or unhealthy self.

Building a healthy ego and becoming the best version of yourself is the ultimate goal of life because it determines whether you have peace of mind or mental chaos. This chapter explains how believing in Serendipity is essential to developing a healthy ego. The way to get the sweet fruits of life is to nourish yourself with care and tenderness.

Only then will you be able to discover the blessings and fortunes that life sends your way. Loving yourself is a form of Serendipity, and it only comes when your relationship with yourself is vital, connected, and aware. I am proud of you for being on Step 2. This shows that you are willing to work on yourself and gather the knowledge you need to become strong enough to tackle and counter the bouts of negativity we all so easily fall prey to.

A strong and connected self can look for the positive and opportunities in every aspect of existence. What do I mean by strong and connected? By being strong, I mean emotionally strong and able to trust yourself. By being connected? I mean knowing who you are and putting the dislodged parts of yourself back into a harmonious whole. In childhood, we split ourselves into many "selves," whether to please friends and family, conform to social and cultural pressure, or meet gender norms. In the process, our true self is shattered like a broken mirror.

Have you ever wondered which piece of the mirror reflects your true self? As you delve deeper into Serendipity and connect with your authentic self, you'll come to realize that no matter how disjointed your various facets may seem, your true essence was never lost.

You are an inseparable part of the cosmic Source, a blend of Goddust and Stardust, and possess an eternal Soul. Through the Shadow Work exercises in this course, you'll learn to piece together your fragmented selves and become whole again.

Once you establish a strong bond with your true self, you'll begin to appreciate your worth and love yourself more, which many people find challenging. This self-love and self-worth will bring incredible joy to your life, and it's one of the most rewarding outcomes of Serendipity. Ultimately, you'll embrace that cultivating a positive mindset is key to unlocking the treasure of self-love and self-worth, and it's not a one-time gift. If you remain committed to this mindset, it will continue to bless your life with positive vibes.

Discovering Serendipity can unearth hidden qualities within yourself that you may have never realized before. Often, we fail to see our true worth, so we never bother to delve deeper into our potential.

Recognizing your value can unlock priceless assets that have the power to transform all aspects of your life.

Self-love is the key to attracting Serendipity into your life. When you train your mind to think positively, you can recognize and seize moments of good fortune and positive energy.

Serendipity is not limited to external occurrences, such as finding people or things. It is also an inner journey that leads you to discover your true self and the unique gifts and hidden treasures that reside within you. Loving yourself takes time and practice, so be gentle with yourself as you explore the depths of your heart and soul.

Discovering serendipitous moments can bring great joy and unexpected surprises. These fleeting moments move quickly and require attentiveness to recognize and seize. With practice, you can develop a perspective that tunes into serendipitous energy and unlocks your full potential.

For instance, trying something new, like cooking, may reveal hidden talents you never knew you had. By taking a courageous step forward and asking yourself, "Am I a good cook?" you may be ecstatic and proud of what you can accomplish.

Uncovering hidden talents is not just a stroke of luck but can also lead to more fortunate occurrences. The positivity that arises from this discovery boosts your self-esteem and enhances your connections with others. People are naturally attracted to those with a strong sense of self-worth, impressed by their confidence and joy.

When you begin the process of healing your fragmented self-image, Serendipity can help you tap into talents and abilities that you may have locked away. As you radiate positivity, you'll attract like-minded people into your life who will bring you happiness, love, trust, and admiration. These encounters may come in surprising and unexpected ways, but they will help you align with your true self and improve your external environment.

These new relationships can have a positive impact on your life by increasing your self-trust and confidence. As you learn to communicate your self-worth, you'll become more confident and attractive. Serendipity is like an infinity loop: the more you embrace her positive energy and take leaps of faith, the more you'll discover unique aspects of yourself and continue to grow.

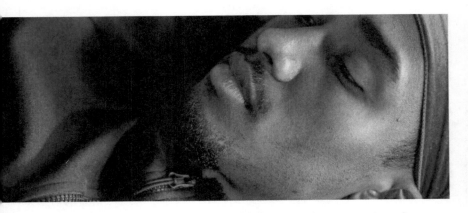

Discovering Serendipity is possible if we remain open to it and appreciate the blessings it brings. Each day presents new opportunities, and as we become more grateful for them, we can confidently anticipate what the future holds.

The relationship between Serendipity and the Self is crucial, as it can bring positive outcomes and the strength to persevere through challenges. Whether spiritual, emotional, or physical, we can overcome any obstacle by recalling moments of positivity and maintaining our focus.

Every day, we encounter situations that require self-love and confidence. Utilizing the "7 Steps To a Life of Serendipity," we can conquer these challenges and diligently pursue our dreams. Trust in yourself and your ability to handle whatever comes your way.

Take some time for yourself and reflect on your life's purpose. This is an act of self-care and productive thinking. Rather than focusing solely on whether you are living up to your potential, ask yourself what you want from life. Consider the moments that have brought you happiness and influenced you in some way. Recall the concept of serendipity discussed in chapter one, and think about its presence in your life.

Look beyond the surface and appreciate the journey while considering its impact on your life. These moments are present in everyone's lives, but it takes a certain awareness to appreciate them truly.

Have you ever noticed the impact of Serendipity in your life? If so, you can attest to the fact that it can help you create a new reality for yourself. Serendipitous events positively influence your mindset, making you feel like you are constantly encountering pleasant surprises.

You can transform your lifestyle and inner self by discovering new things daily. Serendipity can increase your sense of gratitude and instill a sense of anticipation for the surprises that life has in store for you.

The role of Serendipity in your life is crucial. It attracts positive vibes and helps you through challenging times, encouraging you to fight for your dreams. You can probably think of several instances where a serendipitous discovery helped you overcome a difficult situation. Remembering these moments can be beneficial as you tackle new challenges.

Overall, Serendipity can prove to be a fortunate occurrence, particularly under trying circumstances. It can help you breathe a little easier and find the strength to persevere.

Like many instances, serendipity plays a vital role in building one's confidence and shaping their personality. Its benefits can only be recognized when one tunes their mindset with positivity and starts seeking it out in their life.

When one embraces Serendipity, it reciprocates by bringing treasures of hidden qualities and helping them find a peaceful relationship with their inner self. Therefore, always seek out serendipity, as it will keep surprising you in positive ways.

# Shadow Work Subsciption

Blue Tourmaline is a great option if you're looking for a crystal to aid in healing and relaxation during meditation.

Its depths can bring a sense of peace and tranquility, while also helping you recognize and release past hurts. You can keep it with you in your pocket, necklace, or bra.

Additionally, lighting a blue candle during meditation can help you focus on expanding your spirituality and opening your mind to new possibilities.

Imagine the gentle swaying of the ocean as you use the candle to guide your meditation.

# Before you
*begin your Gratitude Journal*

Try practicing these self-affirmations daily for a week to improve your mental well-being. Take note of negative thoughts that hinder your recall of happy memories.

Clear your space and mind by burning a Sage Smudge stick.

Make yourself comfortable and take a deep breath through your nose, filling your belly, and then exhale through your mouth. Repeat twice.

Let's try these self-affirmations. Visualize your own "genuinely surprised" face - yes, YOUR face! You can even try this exercise while sitting in front of a mirror.

Imagine your face when you receive a promotion or meet your soulmate, and they say "I love you" for the first time.

Picture your face when someone you value says they are proud of you or when a stranger spontaneously compliments you.

These are incredible feelings that showcase your unique magic. When you need to connect with yourself, ground yourself by visualizing these moments. It's called grounding in self-love.

# Before you
*begin your Gratitude Journal*

You can experience genuine joy and happiness without sharing it with anyone else. Make it a habit to jot down one positive memory in your daily planner daily. By the end of the week, you'll have seven great moments where you were the hero of your own life.

Let's explore the various aspects of your personality. Create a list that notes how you behave around different people, such as parents, partners, siblings, children, friends, co-workers, neighbors, teachers, employees, service people, and even strangers. Remember to include how you treat yourself when you're alone.

I'd like you to please visualize how you want to act and how you want to be perceived by yourself and others. Once you've accomplished this task, you'll feel a sense of ownership over your true self, which is when self-worth appears. This approach is more concrete and provides a specific task to follow rather than leaving individuals overwhelmed by trying to identify themselves independently.

Scan the QR Code to take you to your daily affirmations.

# Gratitude Journal

s  m  t  w  t  f  s

Date :

My Cards for the day

Today I'm grateful for

Schedule

Hope

- [ ] _____
- [ ] _____
- [ ] _____
- [ ] _____

- [ ] _____
- [ ] _____
- [ ] _____
- [ ] _____

Notes

# Gratitude Journal

s   m   t   w   t   f   s

Date :

### My Cards for the day

### Today I'm grateful for

### Schedule

☐ _____
☐ _____
☐ _____
☐ _____

### Hope

☐ _____
☐ _____
☐ _____
☐ _____

### Notes

# Gratitude Journal

s m t w t f s

Date :

My Cards for the day

Today I'm grateful for

Schedule

☐ _____
☐ _____
☐ _____
☐ _____

Hope

☐ _____
☐ _____
☐ _____
☐ _____

Notes

# Gratitude Journal

s    m    t    w    t    f    s

Date :

My Cards for the day                Today i'm grateful for

Schedule                            Hope

☐ _____    ☐ _____
☐ _____    ☐ _____
☐ _____    ☐ _____
☐ _____    ☐ _____

Notes

# Gratitude Journal

Date :

### My Cards for the day

### Today I'm grateful for

### Schedule

- ☐ _____
- ☐ _____
- ☐ _____
- ☐ _____

### Hope

- ☐ _____
- ☐ _____
- ☐ _____
- ☐ _____

### Notes

# Gratitude Journal

s     m     t     w     t     f     s

Date :

My Cards for the day

Today i'm grateful for

Schedule

☐ _____
☐ _____
☐ _____
☐ _____

Hope

☐ _____
☐ _____
☐ _____
☐ _____

Notes

# Gratitude Journal

s    m    t    w    t    f    s

Date :

### My Cards for the day

### Today I'm grateful for

_____

### Schedule

☐ _____
☐ _____
☐ _____
☐ _____

### Hope

☐ _____
☐ _____
☐ _____
☐ _____

### Notes

# Step 3: Serendipity in Relationship with God

# Serendipity in Relationship with God

Many people hold the belief that a higher power created the universe and governed it based on a predetermined plan. Having faith in God or a universal Source also acknowledges Serendipity's role in this predetermination paradigm. Although we may encounter unexpected events, they are not merely coincidences but rather a part of the plan for our lives.

People experience the joys of Serendipity in various ways, regardless of their awareness. However, if someone does not have faith in a higher power, Serendipity may seem like mere luck or coincidence. On the other hand, if someone believes in God, their perspective on unexplainable events is open-minded, and they recognize something beyond themselves. But how does Serendipity enhance one's relationship with God?

I have a secret to share with you. If you view chance happenings through the lens of belief, finding Serendipity will come naturally. This is because you already have faith in something greater than yourself. The beauty of fortunate events is that they reinforce your trust in God.

Those with a strong relationship with God don't attribute unexpected coincidences to luck, chance, or accident. Instead, they see them as blessings and rewards from their Maker due to their intimate relationship with Him. They believe that God favors them and is committed to helping them in their lives.

On the other hand, people who experience unexpected adverse events see them as God's way of teaching them valuable life lessons. They believe their challenges will ultimately lead to a greater appreciation and worship of God. Regardless of your beliefs, whether in a supernatural being, an omniscient deity, a lifeforce, or the old gods, this study guide encourages you to embrace a life of Serendipity.

Recognizing the power of Serendipity and incorporating this belief into your life can significantly enhance your relationship with God. A strong connection with God or Source is essential to any belief system. Even non-believers learn to analyze events and occurrences within this framework. When faced with difficulty, your optimism is primarily determined by the strength of your relationship with God. A firm connection allows your subconscious to anticipate relief, and positive outcomes will likely follow.

This is how a devout belief in God leads to a belief in Serendipity. By attributing life's successes to divine assistance, individuals who hold supernatural beliefs attract more positive outcomes through meditation or spiritual practices. The Law of Attraction unfolds before them, and they expect good things to come their way without surprise.

You may start to appreciate the small gestures of kindness displayed by people in your daily life and the little miracles that cross your path, such as a butterfly or a baby's laughter. God sends these occurrences to assist, comfort, and guide you. These seemingly insignificant moments are signs from God, reminding you to smile and letting you know He is watching over you.

As you become more aware of them, you will treasure these minor blessings and experience overwhelming joy. Suddenly, you will notice more signs and symbols of joy surrounding you. This will make you grateful to God and strengthen your relationship with Him. As you feel the love of God through these unexpected moments of goodness, you will also share this affection with others.

Have you ever considered why you met someone who makes you happy just when you yearned for company? Or are you wondering why you read these exact words in this eCourse? This moment is not by coincidence. This moment is what you prayed for or even dreamed of. You were searching for this moment, so it was written for you and will help you start your shadow work.

At this very moment, Serendipity is happening. God is helping you escape depression or the idea of being alone by sending someone to help you through it, and I am honored and humbled that God, Goddess, Spirit, and/or Source used me to share these steps with you.

As we progress towards your next steps, you'll notice a positive shift in your outlook on life. You'll become more enthusiastic about people, places, and things because you have a purpose in the world. To discover serendipity, you must know symbols, signals, and signs.

This new adventure will help you appreciate surprises and categorize them as serendipitous moments. Journaling will make more sense as it allows you to document and cherish these moments forever. As you aspire for a content lifestyle, serendipity will provide valuable insights and understanding, ultimately leading to wisdom and knowledge. You'll become more intelligent intuitively.

You can relate many serendipitous events in your life to the kindness of God, who carried you through tough times. It was the result of your strong faith and unwavering relationship with Him. Your heart anticipated help, and it manifested itself in various ways.

Serendipitous events often occur when one strongly connects with God, the Source, and the Universe. This connection is strengthened through faith, which instills a positive outlook and belief in something greater than oneself. A positive attitude can attract both positive and negative energies, leading to unexpected encounters and opportunities in life.

That's how Serendipity operates. Trust in the symbols, signals, and signs. They are yours; these are your guides. No one else has the same ones. They are unique, like your fingerprints. You will see your guides in numbers, words, phrases, cycles, patterns, frequencies, vibrations, and deja vu as you recognize them. The process will give you a balance between positive and negative.

Remember, God created both, and they are a part of you.

To focus on finding your guides, you realize that you have become very aware of your present moment. Because what you need to see might be behind you when you only use your physical eyes. When you tune in to senses, then even a breeze of air or a click of a broken stick under your shoes or a bird chirping or a bus rushing by, all of them become your present, and this moment holds the essence of Serendipity. There is no fear, no projection of what might happen, and no guilt and worry about the past in the present moment. There is only peace in the present moment.

To experience Serendipity, it is essential to live in the present moment. This is where Serendipity can be felt most strongly. It is a nurturing and feminine energy that feels like a warm embrace. It resides in the sixth layer of your aura, which can be researched online. The good news is that you can access this energy anytime. All you need to do is focus on the present moment, calm your mind, cultivate gratitude, and be open to signs and symbols. This mindset acts like a magnet, attracting unexpected blessings into your life.

As your relationship with God strengthens, so does your belief in His serendipitous blessings. To gain a broader understanding of Serendipity, it is essential to acknowledge all of the positivity around you. The positive energy in your relationship with God will be reflected in your attitude, which others will notice. Look for excellence in everything that happens, and believe in God's help and how He assists you.

By embracing every present moment with a focus on excellence, you will increase the Serendipity in your life and feel grateful towards God with every step you take. While we all experience dark days, bad news, loneliness, and uncertainty, Step 1 provides you with tools or weapons to battle negativity. It's not an easy battle, but with the right mindset, it can be won.

When individuals are struggling with depression, they can utilize the tools and techniques learned in the YouTube video titled "Self-Love Affirmations and Calming Turbulent Thoughts."

During difficult times, having a peaceful mind can help you find solutions. You can gain control over your thoughts by commanding negative thoughts to leave your mind, energy, and reality and inviting positive thoughts to enter. Speaking these positive thoughts aloud can lead to a quick shift in energy. Repeating self-love affirmations can transform your energy until your mind is calm. To reinforce your positive mindset, try clapping three times.

It would be a great idea to book an intuitive tarot reading to understand your present circumstances better. Embracing Serendipity as a way of living entails nurturing a positive mindset in tune with healthy emotions and feelings and regularly experiencing the "Feeling of Serendipity." This necessitates mastering your thoughts and emotions to generate a positive energy that becomes a part of your being and remains with you always.

Remember moments when you experienced unexpected success, especially when you felt like you were giving up or were utterly hopeless. These instances of finding something positive during hard times can be helpful to hold onto when you feel like your mental state is declining. Practicing Steps 1 and 2 will help you maintain hope and stay grounded.

These moments of Serendipity can be seen as signs of God's presence. Feeling a sense of help before it appears can indicate an intense and intimate relationship with God.

Everything happens for a reason, so pay attention to the world around you. Please take note of odd comments or things that catch your eye, as they may reappear later in the day or week. Serendipity often appears after a third occurrence, so look for these signs.

# Shadow Work Subsciption

If you're looking for natural ways to purify the energy in your home, consider incorporating selenite, amethyst, black tourmaline, and clear quartz into your decor.

These crystals are known for their ability to cleanse and protect. Additionally, blue aventurine can help promote peace and reduce anxiety.

It's a great option if you're looking for emotional support and mental relief.

# Before you
*begin your Gratitude Journal*

Shall we examine this chart together? It would be beneficial for you to reflect on your emotions and discover ways to alter them. This chart can assist in recognizing the source of your emotions and the reason behind their manifestation.

## Levels of Consciousness Chart

| Dimension, Vibration & Colour | Level of Consciousness | Energetic Frequency | Associated Emotional State | View of Life | Key to Transcending to the Next Level | What We Experience | States of Consciousness | Location |
|---|---|---|---|---|---|---|---|---|
| 12th Dimension | Full Consciousness | 1000 | | | Disappearance of material desires, purpose is effortlessly supported | | Pure Consciousness | |
| | Supra Causal Truth | 900 | | | | | | |
| | Divine Grace & Love | 850 | Ineffable | Is | | | Enlightenment | |
| Enlightenment | The Great Void | 800 | | | | Synchronicity & Extraordinary Outcomes | | Heaven |
| | Awareness | 700 | | | | | Over Mind | |
| I AM Presence | Non-Duality | 670 | | | Allowing | | | |
| 5th Dimension | Presence/Peace | 600 | Bliss | Perfect | | | Illuminated Mind | |
| | Oneness/Joy | 540 | Serenity | Complete | | | | |
| New Humanity Consciousness | Inner Love | 500 | Reverence | Benign | | | Higher Mind | Paradise |
| | Inner Wisdom | 440 | | | Meaning | | Transcendence | |
| | Inner Light/Reason | 400 | Understanding | Meaningful | | | Super Mind | |
| 4th Dimension | Acceptance | 350 | Forgiveness | Harmonious | Stepping out with passion | Happiness & Productivity | Flow | In Between |
| | Willingness | 310 | Optimism | Hopeful | Purpose | | In The Zone (Normal Mind Body State) | |
| | Neutrality | 250 | Trust | Satisfactory | | | Getting By | |
| | Courage | 200 | Affirmation | Feasible | Appreciation | | Narrowed Consciousness | |
| 3rd Dimension | Pride | 175 | Scorn | Demanding | Use energy positively | Hyper-activity | Mental illnesses | Purgatory |
| | Anger | 150 | Hate | Antagonistic | | | | |
| | Desire | 125 | Craving | Disappointing | I am worthy | | Suffering | |
| | Fear | 100 | Anxiety | Frightening | Overcome fear | | Drug Intoxication | |
| | Grief | 75 | Regret | Tragic | | | Out-of-Body Experience, Near-Death Experience, Possession States Unconsciousness REM Sleep Coma Death | |
| | Apathy | 50 | Despair | Hopeless | Take action | Inaction | | Hell |
| | Guilt | 30 | Blame | Evil | | | | |
| | Shame | 20 | Humiliation | Miserable | | | | |
| | Death | 0 | | | | | | |

*LOVE* *FEAR*

# Gratitude Journal

s   m   t   w   t   f   s

Date :

My Cards for the day

Today I'm grateful for

Schedule

- [ ] _____
- [ ] _____
- [ ] _____
- [ ] _____

Hope

- [ ] _____
- [ ] _____
- [ ] _____
- [ ] _____

Notes

# Gratitude Journal

s   m   t   w   t   f   s

Date :

My Cards for the day

Today I'm grateful for

Schedule

☐ _____
☐ _____
☐ _____
☐ _____

Hope

☐ _____
☐ _____
☐ _____
☐ _____

Notes

# Gratitude Journal

s    m    t    w    t    f    s

Date :

My Cards for the day

Today I'm grateful for

Schedule

☐ _____
☐ _____
☐ _____
☐ _____

Hope

☐ _____
☐ _____
☐ _____
☐ _____

Notes

# Gratitude Journal

s    m    t    w    t    f    s

Date :

My Cards for the day

Today I'm grateful for

Schedule

☐ _____
☐ _____
☐ _____
☐ _____

Hope

☐ _____
☐ _____
☐ _____
☐ _____

Notes

# Gratitude Journal

s m t w t f s

Date :

My Cards for the day

Today I'm grateful for

Schedule

☐ _____
☐ _____
☐ _____
☐ _____

Hope

☐ _____
☐ _____
☐ _____
☐ _____

Notes

# Gratitude Journal

s    m    t    w    t    f    s

Date :

My Cards for the day

Today I'm grateful for

Schedule

☐ _____
☐ _____
☐ _____
☐ _____

Hope

☐ _____
☐ _____
☐ _____
☐ _____

Notes

# Step 4:
## Serendipity in Trials & Tribulation

## Serendipity in Trials & Tribulation

Life can be unpredictable and challenging. Even when everything seems to be going well, unexpected obstacles, sickness, and loss can arise. It can feel like you're walking on a bed of thorns instead of being showered with rose petals. These challenges can be difficult to navigate, but they can also provide opportunities for growth and resilience. Remember that these difficulties are temporary and you have the strength to overcome them.

If life were always easy, you wouldn't have the chance to develop mentally and would become emotionally and you would not learn how to overcome adversity.

Without any challenges in your life, you appreciate the moments when things are going well. Moreover, you would become weak, lazy, and complacent. Challenges are a part of life and growing up. They appear when God often needs you to focus on the path he has set for you. If life were to offer you everything without struggle, you could not fully value your special gifts.

61

If life were to offer you everything without struggle, you could not fully value your special gifts.

History shows that humans depend on innate abilities and advantages when faced with difficulties. These challenges are always turned into growth opportunities in combination with a higher power to survive.

The purpose of these tests is to help us value life and develop our inner strength. When you face obstacles, it's a chance to embrace Serendipity and change the trajectory of your life. Remember that trials and tribulations reveal the hidden potential within you and help you discover your inner superpower.

You can discover hidden talents, skills, and strengths that will help you overcome obstacles by challenging yourself beyond your limits. It requires courage to push yourself to the edge, but if you are willing to put in the effort, you will be rewarded with the gift of Serendipity.

When striving for success, viewing yourself as an athlete is essential. Winning a competition isn't simply a matter of showing up - you must consistently improve physically, mentally, and emotionally daily. This practice builds "muscle memory," allowing you to navigate challenging situations easily. With this athlete's mindset, you may feel overwhelmed yet capable and disciplined enough to strive to be the best.

As you approach the end of the chapter, a cognitive exercise awaits you. This exercise will aid you in reviewing every morning, helping alter negative thought patterns and replacing them with positive thinking and behavior patterns. This practice will allow you to problem-solve effectively when facing trials and tribulations. The question, then, is how to discover and embrace Serendipity during trials and tribulations.

It's common to feel isolated and lonely during tough times, leading to depression. However, with Serendipity, you can survive and thrive in these moments. Serendipity equips you with the necessary strength and tools to face more significant challenges, such as patience, persistence, faith, joy, self-confidence, love, and hope.

But it's important to know how to use these tools effectively. You can only overcome challenges when you can use them wisely. When you're facing difficulties, patience is the most effective tool. This may contradict what society says about dealing with tough times, but calmly accepting the uncomfortable feelings you experience is essential for coping with adversity.

Remaining calm does not imply avoiding action when faced with trials. It entails managing your emotions by acknowledging and understanding lousy news as an opportunity for growth, discovering your strengths, and being open to unexpected opportunities. Through it all, it's important to trust that a solution will come from a higher power. Even in the most daunting situations, patience and calmness are essential to test your limits and build resilience. Serendipity teaches us that some things are not worth the energy, and conserving it for what truly matters is important.

Have you ever considered letting life unfold instead of forcing it? It's a valuable lesson I've learned. Please take a moment to sit back and embrace life as it happens. Ask yourself, how can I navigate the path of least resistance? Could I identify my way when it presents itself?

In a serious health diagnosis or experiencing abuse, taking action and seeking professional assistance is crucial. Despite the overwhelming feelings of hopelessness and despair that may arise, it is essential to remember that you can always make choices for your well-being. It is only disabled, children, elderly individuals, and animals who may be genuinely unable to help themselves. Remember, it is possible to prioritize your needs without feeling guilty.

Remaining calm does not imply avoiding action when faced with trials. It entails managing your emotions by acknowledging and understanding lousy news as an opportunity for growth, discovering your strengths, and being open to unexpected opportunities. Through it all, it's important to trust that a solution will come from a higher power. Even in the most daunting situations, patience and calmness are essential to test your limits and build resilience. Serendipity teaches us that some things are not worth the energy, and conserving it for what truly matters is important.

Have you ever considered letting life unfold instead of forcing it? It's a valuable lesson I've learned. Please take a moment to sit back and embrace life as it happens. Ask yourself, how can I navigate the path of least resistance? Could I identify my way when it presents itself?

In a serious health diagnosis or experiencing abuse, taking action and seeking professional assistance is crucial. Despite the overwhelming feelings of hopelessness and despair that may arise, it is essential to remember that you can always make choices for your well-being. It is only disabled, children, elderly individuals, and animals who may be genuinely unable to help themselves. Remember, it is possible to prioritize your needs without feeling guilty.

Remember always to remember Serendipity - it's like a gift from above, a miracle that can give you the strength to overcome obstacles. As we mentioned earlier, your connection with God can help you recognize and be grateful for the small blessings of Serendipity in your everyday life.

Faith in God can be a source of strength when dealing with various situations. It instills a sense of fearlessness, knowing that God's love and support are always present. Relying on this belief can provide the courage to navigate life's challenges.

With strong faith, one can face any tribulation with confidence, viewing them as tests that can make them more resilient. Even in hopeless situations, the knowledge that God will provide blessings and guidance can prevent feelings of dismay. Trusting in God can be a powerful tool for coping with life's ups and downs.

I want to remind you that miracles can come your way to help you overcome any obstacle. It's important to approach life with a positive, loving, and patient attitude toward yourself and others. Repeat the mantra "Fear and Faith Don't Mix" daily to mentally prepare for challenges.

To overcome challenges, it's crucial to avoid succumbing to feelings of depression. Instead, focus on cultivating happiness and optimism. Refrain from dwelling excessively on your problems, which can drain your energy and morale. Stay positive and keep an open mind, as good fortune often favors those who approach life positively. Remember to continue taking the Open Heart Tincture from Chapter 1.

Providing adequate hydration and nutrition is crucial for you to flourish. Neglecting these needs will inevitably result in dis-ease. Similarly, cultivating self-confidence and belief in your abilities is a powerful tool for conquering obstacles. Just as plants require water to thrive, nourishing oneself with positivity and self-assurance can lead to tremendous personal growth.

Life presents numerous challenges, each demanding its own unique attitude and approach to overcome. One must possess mental fortitude and clarity to adopt the appropriate perspective. It is crucial to have tailored strategies for tackling diverse situations.

When facing adversity, it's crucial to maintain a composed mind. Your mental strength is critical in overcoming difficult situations. Prioritizing your mental well-being is key. By cultivating a positive attitude, you increase the chances of experiencing serendipitous moments. A positive outlook also boosts morale and self-confidence, giving you the courage to stay strong and determined during tough times.

In challenging times, self-love and love for others can be powerful weapons to help you cope. By loving yourself, you equip yourself to confront difficulties without losing your sanity. Self-love provides the motivation necessary to overcome tough times. To cultivate a consistent habit of self-love, try practicing some of the examples provided at the end of this chapter throughout the week.

Another source of strength during difficult times is the love of family and friends. Accepting or seeking support from loved ones, support groups, therapists, or coaches can help you navigate trials. When faced with challenging situations, I remind myself to always "try." After all, the worst that can happen is hearing "no."

However, saying "yes" can lead to unexpected opportunities and renewed self-confidence. Serendipity may bring the right people and their support into your life when needed.

If you try by giving just 1% effort toward transforming your life, God will send Serendipity your way to provide you with the remaining 99%. Even if you are not getting tangible help from others, realizing that people believe in you will give you the strength you need to succeed. Having someone to offer moral support can be incredibly beneficial to your morale. If you need more clarification about pursuing something in your life, I highly recommend exploring the resources and support groups; please feel free to contact me for a list of highly recommended therapists.

Hope is a powerful tool for success in times of trouble. Even when the world seems full of doom and gloom, there is always optimism if you train yourself to recognize and embrace it. The media often perpetuates the idea that the world is full of disaster, so consider disconnecting from your TV and social media and instead take in the beauty of nature, which is like God's TV. Connect with people, and you will indeed cross paths with angels. Seek mentors who have achieved the dreams you aspire to and listen to their guidance. This is the essence of Serendipity, and it can bring positive blessings your way. All you need is hope, an inquisitive mind, and an open heart.

If you're wondering what hope is and how to achieve peace of mind, remember that hope and peace of mind are separate concepts from self-love, joy, and happiness.

# Shadow Work Subsciption

If you're looking for natural ways to purify the energy in y
home, consider incorporating selenite, amethyst, black tourma
and clear quartz into your decor.

These crystals are known for their ability to cleanse and pro
Additionally, blue aventurine can help promote peace and rec
anxiety.

It's a great option if you're looking for emotional support
mental relief.

# Before you
## begin your Gratitude Journal

Can you imagine being wrongly imprisoned for over 30 years? Scan the QR code and hear his testimony.
It sheds light on his discovery of his fate and the injustice he has endured. The Georgia Innocence Project has taken on his case, and we eagerly await updates on his serendipitous journey toward justice and home to be with his loved ones.

Review this cognitive exercise every morning to equip yourself with the tools of Serendipity. Before bed, repeat the exercise to embed these words in your third eye chakra.

"Even when feeling low, I can use my weapons to overcome daily challenges. Listening to self-doubts will only hinder my progress."

"I deserve credit for not giving in to my negative thoughts. Every time I face a challenge, I securely reach for one of my spiritual weapons; I deserve to feel self-confidence and joy."

"I need to practice patience, mindfulness, and self-kindness when facing difficult challenges."

"Setting boundaries with others when their expectations hinder my ability to face the day is okay. Communicating those boundaries nicely but assertively serves my higher self. It's better to disappoint them than to disappoint myself."

"I will avoid or minimize interactions with people who bring negative energy into my life."

# Gratitude Journal

s    m    t    w    t    f    s

Date :

My Cards for the day

Today I'm grateful for

Schedule

☐ _____
☐ _____
☐ _____
☐ _____

Hope

☐ _____
☐ _____
☐ _____
☐ _____

Notes

# Gratitude Journal

s    m    t    w    t    f    s

Date :

My Cards for the day

Today I'm grateful for

Schedule

☐ _____
☐ _____
☐ _____
☐ _____

Hope

☐ _____
☐ _____
☐ _____
☐ _____

Notes

# Gratitude Journal

| s | m | t | w | t | f | s |
|---|---|---|---|---|---|---|

Date :

My Cards for the day

Today i'm grateful for

Schedule

☐ _____

☐ _____

☐ _____

☐ _____

Hope

☐ _____

☐ _____

☐ _____

☐ _____

Notes

# Gratitude Journal

s    m    t    w    t    f    s

Date :

My Cards for the day

Today I'm grateful for

_____
_____
_____
_____
_____
_____
_____

_____
_____
_____
_____
_____
_____
_____

Schedule

☐ _____
☐ _____
☐ _____
☐ _____

Hope

☐ _____
☐ _____
☐ _____
☐ _____

Notes

# Gratitude Journal

s    m    t    w    t    f    s

Date :

| My Cards for the day | Today i'm grateful for |
|---|---|

Schedule

Hope

☐ _____    ☐ _____
☐ _____    ☐ _____
☐ _____    ☐ _____
☐ _____    ☐ _____

Notes

# Gratitude Journal

s    m    t    w    t    f    s

Date :

My Cards for the day

Today i'm grateful for

Schedule

☐ _____
☐ _____
☐ _____
☐ _____

Hope

☐ _____
☐ _____
☐ _____
☐ _____

Notes

# Gratitude Journal

Date :

### My Cards for the day

............................................................

............................................................

............................................................

............................................................

............................................................

............................................................

............................................................

............................................................

### Today i'm grateful for

............................................................

............................................................

............................................................

............................................................

............................................................

............................................................

............................................................

............................................................

### Schedule

- [ ] _____
- [ ] _____
- [ ] _____
- [ ] _____

### Hope

- [ ] _____
- [ ] _____
- [ ] _____
- [ ] _____

### Notes

# Step 5: Opening Your Heart to Serendipity

# Creating an Open Heart for Serendipity

Serendipity and the heart have a long and deep connection, for the heart is the first to recognize and accept Serendipity. A heart that is at peace is essential to attaining a peaceful life and peace of mind; you have Serendipity only when your heart is open to welcoming and loving it. Since Serendipity frequently occurs for people with sincere and pure hearts,

To attract Serendipity into your life, it is essential to cleanse your mind of negative thoughts and emotions. Only a pure heart that is open to receiving and cherishing life's blessings can truly experience Serendipity. However, it is possible for even the most sincere and pure heart to miss out on opportunities for Serendipity if they fail to recognize and accept them.

Sometimes, the heart finds it hard to recover from past hurts fully. When these wounds leave behind scars, they can breed a negative mindset that hinders you from relishing the beauty of unexpected moments. A heart encumbered by negative energy cannot readily embrace the positives in life, making it challenging to experience gratitude and contentment.

It is imperative to heal both wounds and scars so that your inner energy can become unblemished and receptive to the joys of life. This way, you can magnetize the serendipitous moments that render life worthwhile.

Discovering and exploring the "heart chakra" can help you open your heart and embrace positive energies. This chakra, located near the heart, governs love, passion, empathy, forgiveness, compassion, trust, and fearlessness in the face of challenges.

By understanding its role, you can become more self-aware of your emotions, how they affect you, and how they shape your relationships with others. This emotional intelligence allows you to heal your inner energy, and prevent future wounds from festering, and close you off to serendipitous experiences. As a result, you'll be able to welcome vibrant and cheerful vibes into your life.

Have you ever thought about the trash bag you disposed of last Tuesday? Can you recall its contents? Do you still feel attached to those items you hastily threw out before they became a breeding ground for flies or emitted a foul odor?

Similarly, when you are overwhelmed with racing thoughts, it's crucial to recognize that some thoughts can be discarded and forgotten forever.

A practical exercise for decluttering your mind is quite simple - start by vocalizing, "I will not dwell on that thought anymore!" or "I no longer need to think about that!" or "That thought has been disposed of like trash, and I have found a solution to it. It does not require my attention!"

If you're still holding onto a negative encounter that occurred years ago, imagine that memory as a bag of trash sitting in your home for two years. As you begin to identify and discard negative thoughts, take a moment to reflect on the relief and clarity that comes with letting go.

Having too many thoughts can become overwhelming and affect our reality. In such situations, guided meditations can be extremely helpful in clearing our minds of negative thoughts. Seeking support from a licensed therapist can also provide a safe space to sort through our thoughts. Building confidence in oneself is crucial, and therapy is a healthy way to take secure steps toward healing. This realization can only be attained by tuning our mindset with positivity. When we start seeking positivity in life and embrace Serendipity, it reciprocates by bringing hidden treasures and helping us find peace within ourselves. Therefore, always seek out Serendipity, which will surprise you positively.

As you read on, you'll understand that Serendipity cannot exist within a broken, grieving, or vengeful heart. It is crucial to heal our hearts as we begin our journey toward successful inner healing. Only then can we truly appreciate the beauty of Serendipity.

To truly understand Serendipity and allow it to enter your life, it's crucial to let go of hostile behavior towards yourself and others. Negative Energy is fueled by fear, worry, guilt, anger, envy, and jealousy, so it's essential to identify and eliminate any sources of negativity in your life, whether they come from negative people, environments, or self-talk.

Take a moment to reflect on situations that bring negative vibrations into your life and write them down. Next, let's focus on opening the heart chakra, which is located in the middle of the ribcage. Incorporate the exercises from previous chapters into your daily practice to help you in your spiritual journey.

Art is like the icing on the cake. It engages all your senses and can help you find freedom and focus. Art is a form of expression that can be abstract, bold, experimental, different, and adventurous. These qualities attract positive energy and good fortune (Law of Attraction). Serendipity is drawn to colors, music, dance, and creativity.

The previous chapter, "Serendipity in Relation with God," explained that God often provides stepping stones to help us navigate the trials and tribulations discussed in Chapter 4. This chapter focuses on the idea that your heart is the key to unlocking Serendipity, one of God's most valuable gifts.

Serendipity, bestowed upon us by God, reveals hidden qualities that we may have never discovered otherwise. These qualities can become invaluable assets, transforming every aspect of our lives. That's why it's crucial to heal your heart chakra to manifest your goals and expand your heart.

Exploring your heart chakra is essential if you wish to embrace Serendipity. Once you take the first step in healing your fragmented mirror pieces, Serendipity can elevate you suddenly to new levels of vibrations. You'll become the person emanating positive vibes in any room! Furthermore, Serendipity will introduce you to like-minded and like-energy people who will effortlessly bring you joy, love, trust, and admiration.

These encounters may come to you in surprising and unexpected ways, which is part of the magic of Serendipity.

Entering into the world of Serendipity is like unlocking a never-ending cycle of positivity. Once you take the first step, you'll experience personal growth, take risks, and uncover new parts of yourself. This, in turn, will boost your self-esteem and confidence, leading you to achieve even more remarkable things.

Serendipity's gifts are bountiful - you may find fortune, success, recognition, and love. Take some time to reflect on your purpose in life. Are you living up to your full potential? What are your aspirations? As you ponder the role of Serendipity in your life, consider her existence, read between the lines, and appreciate the journey. Embrace the process and look for her impact on your life.

Always remember, Serendipity happens to everyone. All you have to do is open yourself up to the possibilities and appreciate what she offers. Every day, you'll discover something new, and as the blessings of Serendipity increase, you'll find yourself looking forward to the future with confidence, embracing whatever surprises it may bring.

Reflecting on your life's purpose is an act of self-love that can bring immense value. It presents an opportunity for productive thinking and helps you focus on what you truly want from life. Take a moment to remember the instances that brought you joy and significantly impacted your life.

Consider the concept of Serendipity from chapter one will contemplate its existence in your life, acknowledging the journey, embracing the process, and reflecting on how it has influenced your life.

Serendipity is a gift that everyone experiences, but only a few can recognize its blessings. Every day presents a chance to explore something new that affects your inner self and lifestyle. As you delve deeper into self-discovery, the power of Serendipity increases your gratitude and anticipation for the surprises life has in store for you.

The role of Serendipity in your life is crucial. It attracts positive energy and helps you navigate through difficult situations. Trust in the power of Serendipity and embrace the journey toward your true purpose.

Becoming confident in oneself requires the fortunate occurrence of Serendipity, which has the power to shape one's personality and provide benefits in many areas. However, to fully appreciate these advantages, individuals must cultivate a positive mindset and actively seek positivity while embracing Serendipity's benefits. This approach will unveil hidden qualities and foster a peaceful relationship with one's inner self, leading to consistent experiences of surprise and positivity brought about by cultivating Serendipity.

# Shadow Work Subsciption

## HOW TO HEAL + OPEN
# HEART CHAKRA

### Blocked Heart Chakra Leads to

Broken heart, unhappiness, loneliness, insecurity, hurt, or inability to receive love.

Leading with the head and not the heart, growing distant from others and putting up walls, shutting down emotionally, or holding onto resentment or bitterness.

### Yoga Poses

- bow pose
- camel pose
- chest openers

### Lifestyle Changes

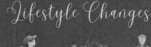

Hiking, eating and wearing greens.

### Oil & Crystals

Bergamot, jasmine, geranium, lavender, cypress, and rose. Amazonite, Emerald, Malachite, and Peridot.

### Affirmations

- I am worthy and deserving of love.
- I forgive myself and others.
- I am open to giving and receiving love.
- I live with gratitude and generosity.
- I honor the guiding of my heart.

### Just Breathe

# Before you
*begin your Gratitude Journa*

"Protect your inner peace" was spoken by one of my closest friends, BRIXX, who has been my most loving support and grounding figure for over 25 years. It would be crazy not to share her keen insight on your heart space.

Here are some simple tips to bring balance back to your heart chakra if it becomes blocked.

1. Express gratitude by keeping a journal and writing down three things you're thankful for each day.

2. Practice backbends, starting with gentle ones like Bhujangasana (Cobra Pose) and moving on to more intense ones like:
Urdhva Mukha Svanasana (Upward-Facing Dog Pose),
Setu Bandha Sarvangasana (Bridge Pose),
Matsyasana (Fish Pose),
Karatkatasana (Wild Thing),
Dhanurasana (Bow Pose), and
Ustrasana (Camel Pose) once you're warmed up.
Scan the QR Code to learn the basic poses. Be Kind to yourself, and don't give up. Yoga and meditation are now part of your tool kit.

3. Try Love and kindness meditations.

4. Wear heart-opening crystals such as rose quartz or place them under your pillow while you sleep. Buy a Dreamcatcher.

5. Consume heart-opening beverages such as rose tea and cacao.

6. Practice affirmations that focus on opening your heart.

# Gratitude Journal

s m t w t f s

Date :

### My Cards for the day

### Today i'm grateful for

### Schedule

- ☐ _____
- ☐ _____
- ☐ _____
- ☐ _____

### Hope

- ☐ _____
- ☐ _____
- ☐ _____
- ☐ _____

### Notes

# Gratitude Journal

s m t w t f s

Date :

My Cards for the day

Today i'm grateful for

Schedule

Hope

Notes

# Gratitude Journal

Date :

### My Cards for the day

### Today i'm grateful for

_____
_____
_____
_____
_____
_____
_____
_____

### Schedule

☐ _____
☐ _____
☐ _____
☐ _____

### Hope

☐ _____
☐ _____
☐ _____
☐ _____

### Notes

# Gratitude Journal

Date :

### My Cards for the day

### Today i'm grateful for

### Schedule

- [ ] _____
- [ ] _____
- [ ] _____
- [ ] _____

### Hope

- [ ] _____
- [ ] _____
- [ ] _____
- [ ] _____

### Notes

#  Gratitude Journal

s    m    t    w    t    f    s

Date :

### My Cards for the day

### Today i'm grateful for

_____

_____

_____

_____

_____

_____

_____

_____

### Schedule

☐ _____

☐ _____

☐ _____

☐ _____

### Hope

☐ _____

☐ _____

☐ _____

☐ _____

### Notes

# Gratitude Journal

s    m    t    w    t    f    s

Date :

### My Cards for the day

### Today i'm grateful for

### Schedule

- [ ] _____
- [ ] _____
- [ ] _____
- [ ] _____

### Hope

- [ ] _____
- [ ] _____
- [ ] _____
- [ ] _____

### Notes

# Gratitude Journal

s m t w t f s

Date :

### My Cards for the day

### Today i'm grateful for

_____
_____
_____
_____
_____
_____
_____
_____
_____

### Schedule

### Hope

☐ _____
☐ _____
☐ _____
☐ _____

☐ _____
☐ _____
☐ _____
☐ _____

### Notes

# Step 6:
## Understanding the Kinship of Serendipity, Blessings, and Miracles

## Step 6:
## Understanding the Kinship of Serendipity, Blessings, and Miracles

You are likely acquainted with the concept of Serendipity and the various blessings, emotions, and experiences it brings into your life. Through this style guide, you have gained a deeper comprehension of how Serendipity has positively influenced you.

In the past, you may have considered instances of significant Serendipity to be miracles, as they seemed to occur unexpectedly, in ways that were advantageous to you or others. It's natural to desire and pray for good outcomes during tough and stressful times.

Therefore, when an unforeseen yet desirable breakthrough occurs, you might refer to it as a miracle or a blessing. Many believe that when something positive happens, it's not just a coincidence but a result of intentionality - whether from God or fate. Once again, Some people may refer to this as a miracle or a blessing. Understanding the difference between these two concepts is important.

To fully grasp the relationship between Serendipity and miracles/blessings. A miracle is a rare and life-altering event that can be experienced by anyone, even those who are feeling pessimistic or depressed. Blessings constantly surround you; it takes only a positive and receptive heart to recognize and appreciate them. These blessings have the power to transform your life, albeit in subtle and gradual ways - almost like miracles.

Your daily existence is filled with countless blessings that bring joy and fulfillment. You are truly blessed when you have friends who support you, a stable career, a shoulder to lean on during tough times, and sufficient resources to live comfortably and securely. However, it's easy to take these gifts for granted and focus on what we need rather than remembering to appreciate the abundance we already possess.

Unfortunately, we often overlook our blessings and place our hopes on miracles when faced with adversity or challenging situations. Instead of searching for solutions within our pot of blessings - where they usually lie - we hope miracles rescue us. But let's be honest: it's easier to hope for a miracle that requires no effort on our part than to do the work. Most challenges and tough situations are tackled by practicing self-care, addressing past hurts, having a heart open to positivity, and tapping into the people and resources in our lives (both those already in it and those we meet through Serendipity).

There is no rhyme or reason why we should feel like only a miracle can help us find the capacity to turn things in our favor and achieve peace of mind.

I am not saying everything is an illusion of your mind—physical ailments and mental illnesses are real. But there is a difference between mental health and mental illness: mental health is our emotional and social well-being, how we think, feel, and act, whereas mental illness is a medical disorder such as major clinical depression or schizophrenia. If you are dealing with a mental illness, you should always seek professional help immediately, just as you would if you had a broken bone, skin condition, joint pain, or a disease in one of your organs.

Doctors, therapists, and counselors are blessings, so reach out and accept the help they can give you. We are so blessed to live in a world with professionals who have access to centuries of knowledge about the human body and mind and can direct you to the appropriate physical or medication therapies to help you. You are also welcome to contact me directly or navigate to the resources page for some organizations you can get in touch with in addition to your healthcare professional.

The relationship between Serendipity, miracles, and blessings is intimate. Serendipity acts as the younger sibling of Miracle and the sidekick of Blessings. Serendipity occurs when time, space, and people unexpectedly intersect, leading to outcomes ranging from a miracle to a smaller-scale but helpful blessing. For example, if you receive a cancer diagnosis, and after considering your treatment options, you decide to get a second opinion, Serendipity may come into play.

By conducting thorough research and seeking recommendations from your circle, you can put in 20%. God will meet you with 80%, sending Serendipity to connect you with a doctor who knows of a recently approved experimental medication. This new treatment option may succeed where conventional methods provide only a tiny chance of a positive outcome, making this a miracle, with Serendipity playing a significant role.

Having a job that provides financial stability and takes a toll on your physical and emotional well-being is possible. If you find yourself struggling, it's okay to ask for help. Sometimes, unexpected encounters can lead to opportunities for growth and improvement.

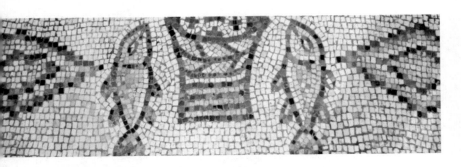

By being open and honest about your concerns and goals, you may find a path that matches your skill set and fulfills your financial and emotional needs. It's essential to remain open to new possibilities and allow Serendipity to guide you toward a brighter future.

Unexpected moments of good fortune, known as Serendipity, can bring positivity into your life each day, no matter how small the outcome. It connects you to miracles and blessings. To live a fulfilled life, recognizing and embracing the concept of Serendipity is vital. Believing in its existence is necessary to notice and take hold of these opportunities, especially during challenging times. This belief will empower you to see the light amidst the darkness, carrying an unwavering torch of hope within you. Maintaining optimism in the face of adversity allows you to identify Serendipity as it comes your way.

There may be moments when you feel lost and directionless, like a ship lost at sea with no land in sight. Those who do not embrace the idea of Serendipity may fall into despair and feel trapped. However, Serendipity can precisely guide you to the right path during these times.

In times of hardship, it can be a comfort to experience unexpected moments of good fortune, miracles, or serendipitous events. These can serve as a glimmer of hope that helps us persevere through tough challenges and tests in life. Individuals who acknowledge and value these positive occurrences often live happier lives. We can trust that difficult periods will eventually end by maintaining a hopeful outlook.

Blessings and miracles may be considered divine gifts for those with religious beliefs during challenging times. However, some may believe these gifts are only granted if we ask for divine intervention through prayer and meditation. This belief implies that pain and suffering are essential for personal growth and that we must plead for relief from a higher power. I do not intend to be impolite to those who hold these beliefs but to present an alternative viewpoint on faith as a journey that does not necessitate begging for blessings and miracles.

If you fail to acknowledge blessings, you will feel gloom and distress. You do not anticipate any good; even when encountering Serendipity, you fail to identify her, and her energy goes to waste.

I believe that consistent prayer and meditation are essential for developing a solid relationship with God. Through these practices, we engage in conversations with God that form the foundation of a deep and meaningful connection. By quieting the world's noise and turning inward, we can share our positive and negative emotions with God and gain a new perspective on ourselves. This helps us connect with God and understand our true selves. As we learn to trust in God, we also build trust in ourselves, creating a solid and lasting bond that withstands life's challenges.

This trust creates a sense of heightened awareness as we remain open to the possibility of serendipitous moments in all aspects of life. Whether facing challenges, practicing self-care, experiencing heartache or triumph, maintaining a positive outlook, and seeking God's gifts, help us move forward with grace and resilience. It allows us to forgive those who wronged us, seek counseling, and expand our knowledge through reading. By continually seeking Serendipity, we can live purposefully and meaningfully.

Serendipity showers you with life's gifts boosts your morale, and lifts you so you are ready for hardships. When you see hope extending a hand toward you, you discover your inner strength and the courage to get up and fight. To remind you, your attitude determines whether or not you will be attracting the gifts of Serendipity.

It can be difficult to maintain hope when your heart feels heavy with darkness. However, by actively cultivating a sense of positivity, you can live a fulfilling and joyful life. Always remember that you can bring light into your heart and create a life full of serendipitous moments.

Your unwavering trust in yourself is evident in your consistent pursuit of Serendipity. This tenacious mindset of always seeking the unexpected good, even amid challenging times, self-care, heartbreak, or success and good times, is a powerful tool that keeps you positive and moving forward. It also empowers you to forgive those who wronged you, seek therapy, and expand your horizons through reading. By persistently pursuing Serendipity, you no longer need to chase, plead or beg after anything else. You can exist and relish the moment.

# Shadow Work Subsciption

When it comes to attracting positive energy and repelling negative energy, Shungite is a great choice. Incorporating it into your life can shift your energy field and attract more abundance and good luck. Shungite can balance all chakras, focusing on the root chakra, which helps you stay grounded and aligned with your life goals. Keeping Shungite in your home and wearing it close to your skin at all times is recommended to ward off negativity. Remember to affirm positivity, good luck, and abundance in your life.

Black candles and a few cloves are useful for absorbing negative energy, strengthening your inner self, protecting yourself, and eliminating evil spirits. They are especially beneficial for candle magic or manifestations.

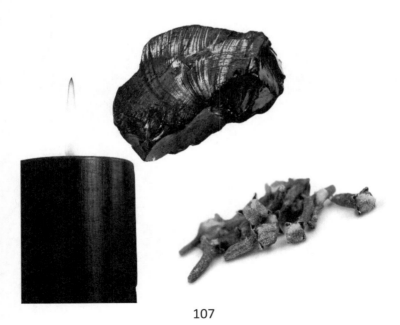

# Before you
## *begin your Gratitude Journal*

Repeat this affirmation when you need to remind yourself of your worth:

"I am Serendipity, Baby!
Serendipity is not just my name,
It's an energy that surrounds me.
- I am Serendipity - is my daily mantra.
Even during my darkest moments,
Or at the height of my success,
And during times of heartbreak,
I am blessed with miracles and abundance."

# Gratitude Journal

s m t w t f s

Date :

### My Cards for the day

### Today i'm grateful for

### Schedule

☐ _____
☐ _____
☐ _____
☐ _____

### Hope

☐ _____
☐ _____
☐ _____
☐ _____

### Notes

# Gratitude Journal

s   m   t   w   t   f   s

Date :

My Cards for the day

Today I'm grateful for

Schedule

☐ _____
☐ _____
☐ _____
☐ _____

Hope

☐ _____
☐ _____
☐ _____
☐ _____

Notes

# Gratitude Journal

s    m    t    w    t    f    s

Date :

### My Cards for the day

### Today i'm grateful for

### Schedule

- ☐ _____
- ☐ _____
- ☐ _____
- ☐ _____

### Hope

- ☐ _____
- ☐ _____
- ☐ _____
- ☐ _____

### Notes

# Gratitude Journal

s  m  t  w  t  f  s

Date :

My Cards for the day

Today i'm grateful for

Schedule

- [ ] _____
- [ ] _____
- [ ] _____
- [ ] _____

Hope

- [ ] _____
- [ ] _____
- [ ] _____
- [ ] _____

Notes

# Gratitude Journal

s m t w t f s

Date :

### My Cards for the day

### Today i'm grateful for

### Schedule

- ☐ _____
- ☐ _____
- ☐ _____
- ☐ _____

### Hope

- ☐ _____
- ☐ _____
- ☐ _____
- ☐ _____

### Notes

# Gratitude Journal

s m t w t f s

Date :

### My Cards for the day

### Today i'm grateful for

### Schedule

- [ ] _____
- [ ] _____
- [ ] _____
- [ ] _____

### Hope

- [ ] _____
- [ ] _____
- [ ] _____
- [ ] _____

### Notes

# Gratitude Journal

s    m    t    w    t    f    s

Date :

My Cards for the day

Today i'm grateful for

Schedule

☐ _____
☐ _____
☐ _____
☐ _____

Hope

☐ _____
☐ _____
☐ _____
☐ _____

Notes

# Step 7:
## I am Serendipity, Baby!

## I am Serendipity, Baby

Greetings! This is Serendipity. By now, you should have a good understanding of my identity from reading this book. Let's recap: Who am I? Have you been able to learn how to recognize me and apply my principles in your life? It's time to look at life from my point of view, through the lens of Serendipity. Many of you have encountered me unexpectedly. I'm like an unannounced guest, but I always bring gifts, just like a gracious visitor should.

These gifts are designed for you and aim to support you during challenging moments. The good news is that I am not only around during difficult times but also moments of happiness when I bring gifts that enhance your joy. Unfortunately, many individuals fail to acknowledge my presence and pass me by without a second thought. I am drawn to those who welcome me with an open heart.

I always seem to be in the right place at the right time, but it's not just a coincidence. Fate and a higher power guide me to you. I appear in the small details of life as well as significant moments. Sometimes, I manifest in nature, like sunshine breaking through clouds or rain on a hot day. The colorful flowers and greenery around you are my way of bringing joy to your day. Whenever you feel happy from these simple pleasures, I lift your spirits.

I've been around for a long time, and my name comes from a Persian folktale about the Emperor of Serendip and his sons. Their success was due to their immediate embrace and appreciation of me. Throughout their journey, I assisted them in achieving great things. Since then, I have continued to help humans reach their goals.

I pride myself on my impeccable timing, always appearing when you need me the most. However, my effectiveness is heavily influenced by your spiritual beliefs and the purity of your heart. While both believers and non-believers can benefit from God's guidance, those who recognize the role of faith in my assistance are more likely to appreciate and benefit from my presence in their lives.

I am the universe's light that illuminates your path. I reveal the bigger picture, showing how your wishes, dreams, goals, and struggles are vital to your success. Some may attribute my actions to God's mysterious ways, but I, Serendipity, am simply a vessel through which God brings positivity into your life. My blessings are meant to bring you happiness that lasts a lifetime. My purpose is to spread joy in unique and unexpected ways.

Treating me like any other guest is necessary if you wish to welcome me into your life. I hold the key to a grateful, enlightened, and receptive heart, but only if you open the door for me. There are numerous ways to make your heart my home and enhance my visit. Have you ever considered why positivity appeals to you when you are happy? It's because when your mind is attuned to positivity, you attract happiness, presence, peace, and serenity into your life.

It is said that a heart that warmly welcomes blessings is bound to attract them. As you learn to cherish the love that flows from within, blessings come your way, and where there are blessings, miracles can happen too. Like a loving family, I am closely related to blessings and miracles. We are always in touch with each other and come to you as messengers of your destiny, sent by God to help you live your life to the fullest.

Perfection may be elusive, but with a positive outlook, you can shape your reality and come close. I am here to guide you on your journey of self-discovery, and I have faith in your ability to believe in yourself and transform your destiny from within. Keep your spirits high and your hopes soaring, for hope is the key to unlocking the power of transformation.

Your adaptability and unwavering positivity in even the darkest times are admirable. You understand that help will eventually present itself, and your hope never falters. Your trust in me strengthens our bond, and I am always here for you, serving as a constant source of light and motivation.

You may have dismissed my work as a mere coincidence in the past, but the truth is that there is a causative agent at work behind every serendipitous moment. Trust in yourself and the universe, and you will witness blessings in unexpected ways. Together, we can conquer anything that comes our way.

As Serendipity, I bring you the gift of self-value and appreciation. You may refer to me as a pleasant surprise, unexpected joy, happy coincidence, or a fortuitous twist of fate, but these labels are just different versions of me. You know me well, and I am here to enrich your life in every way possible.

# Shadow Work Subsciption

Peach Moonstone - This gemstone is known as the stone of serendipity and intuition. Worn to encourage the wearer that everything will work out on your behalf and utmost satisfaction.

Yellow candle is associated with sunshine, hope, laughter, warmth, happiness, and energy. Yellow is found to make a person feel spontaneous and happy. A splash of yellow on anything dull or dark can make a person feel cheerful and optimistic.

What energy does yellow bring? Embrace radiance by placing Sunflowers as Symbols of Spiritual Growth and Enlightenment in your work and living space. " In the presence of sunflowers, you ignite a light within and begin blooming with a purpose. Sunflowers are symbols of spiritual enlightenment, positivity, and personal development, as they turn their faces toward the sun and represent growth and illumination.

# Before you
*begin your Gratitude Journal*

## CHAKRA GUIDE

| CHAKRA | Root | Sacral | Solar Plexus | Heart | Throat | Third-Eye | Crown |
|---|---|---|---|---|---|---|---|
| LOCATION | Base Of Spine | Lower Abdomen | Stomach | Heart | Throat | Forehead | Top of the Head |
| ELEMENT | Earth | Water | Fire | Air | Ether | Light | Consciousne |
| SOUND | LAM | VAM | RAM | YAM | HAM | AUM (Om) | AH |
| EMOTIONS | Safety, security | Sexuality, desire, pleasure | Personal power, purpose | Balance, love | Self-expression, expansion, healing | Intuition, imagination | Bliss, spiritualit |
| BODY | Spine, rectum, legs, arms, circulatory system | Reproductive organs, kidneys, bowels, immune system | Central nervous system, pancreas, liver, skin, digestive tract | Heart, thymus, lower lungs, circulatory system, immune system | Throat, respiratory system, teeth, vocal chords, thyroid | pituitary gland, pineal gland, eyes, brain, sinuses | mind |
| BALANCED BEHAVIOUR | Safe, secure, centered, grounded, happy to be alive | Passion, creative, healthy libido, optimistic, open | Confident, in control, optimistic, ambitious, joyful, easy-going | Generous, loving, compassionate, peaceful, open, empathetic | Expressive, good communicator, trustworthy, calm, honest | Intuitive, faithful, imaginative, integrous, clarity of mind | Connected, present, wise, universal love |
| BLOCKED BEHAVIOUR | Fearful, anxious, insecure, self-pity, self-doubt, aggressive | Low libido, fear of intimacy, aloof, destructive, dependent | Low self-esteem, powerless, pessimistic, over analytical | Lack of empathy, bitter, hateful, trust issues, bitter, jealous | Can't express self, secretive, quiet, shy, moody, not good listener | Poor judgement, lacks focus, poor imagination, depressed | Learning difficulti disconnected from reality, ange lack of faith |
| OVERACTIVE BEHAVIOUR | Greedy, lust for power, aggressive, materialistic, cynical | Over emotional, fixated on sex, hedonistic, manipulative | Power hungry, domineering, perfectionist, critical | Jealous, self sacrificing, codependent, give too much | Opinionated, loud, critical, gossipy, interrupt, harsh words | Nightmares, delusions, hallucinations, obsessive | Dogmatic, judgemental, ungrounded, spiritual addictio |
| FOODS TO HEAL | Beets, parsnips, apples, rutabagas, pomegranates, protein | Beets, parsnips, apples, rutabagas, pomegranates, protein | Yellow peppers, yellow lentils, bananas, oats, corn, squash | Spinach, broccoli, kale, peas, other leafy greens | Blueberries, blue raspberries, kelp, figs | Purple potatoes, blackberries, plums, purple grapes | Fresh air, sunlight, nature |

# Gratitude Journal

s    m    t    w    t    f    s

Date :

### My Cards for the day

### Today i'm grateful for

### Schedule

☐ _____
☐ _____
☐ _____
☐ _____

### Hope

☐ _____
☐ _____
☐ _____
☐ _____

### Notes

# Gratitude Journal

Date :

## My Cards for the day

_____
_____
_____
_____
_____
_____
_____

## Today i'm grateful for

_____
_____
_____
_____
_____
_____
_____

## Schedule

☐ _____
☐ _____
☐ _____
☐ _____

## Hope

☐ _____
☐ _____
☐ _____
☐ _____

## Notes

# Gratitude Journal

s    m    t    w    t    f    s

Date :

### My Cards for the day

### Today i'm grateful for

### Schedule

- [ ] _____
- [ ] _____
- [ ] _____
- [ ] _____

### Hope

- [ ] _____
- [ ] _____
- [ ] _____
- [ ] _____

### Notes

# Gratitude Journal

s    m    t    w    t    f    s

Date :

### My Cards for the day

### Today i'm grateful for

### Schedule

- [ ] _____
- [ ] _____
- [ ] _____
- [ ] _____

### Hope

- [ ] _____
- [ ] _____
- [ ] _____
- [ ] _____

### Notes

# Gratitude Journal

s    m    t    w    t    f    s

Date :

My Cards for the day                    Today i'm grateful for

_____                 _____
_____                 _____
_____                 _____
_____                 _____
_____                 _____
_____                 _____
_____                 _____
_____                 _____
_____                 _____

Schedule                                Hope

☐ _____                 ☐ _____
☐ _____                 ☐ _____
☐ _____                 ☐ _____
☐ _____                 ☐ _____

Notes

# Gratitude Journal

s m t w t f s

Date :

My Cards for the day

Today i'm grateful for

Schedule

Hope

Notes

# Gratitude Journal

s  m  t  w  t  f  s

Date :

My Cards for the day

Today i'm grateful for

Schedule

☐ _____
☐ _____
☐ _____
☐ _____

Hope

☐ _____
☐ _____
☐ _____
☐ _____

Notes

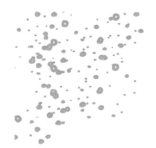

# I Am Serendipity

Meet Susan Dilworth, aka Serendipity - an experienced advisor with tarot, astrology, and herbalism expertise. She offers unique men and women restorative health programs, spiritual mentoring, performance coaching, and tarot readings.

Serendipity's seven-week transformational journal, "7 Steps to a Life of Serendipity," guides individuals in bringing serenity into their lives, allowing them to appreciate the miracle of life and bring them closer to God. By living a Life of Serendipity, people can unexpectedly receive valuable insights that open up a treasure box of emotional, physical, and material contentment.

Made in the USA
Columbia, SC
03 April 2024

33714712R00076